The Forsaken Little Black Book

The Forsaken Little Black Book

Poems by

Julie T. Standig

© 2022 Julie T. Standig. All rights reserved.
This material may not be reproduced in any form, published,
reprinted, recorded, performed, broadcast,
rewritten or redistributed without
the explicit permission of Julie T. Standig.
All such actions are strictly prohibited by law.

Cover design by Shay Culligan
Cover photograph by Julie T. Standig

ISBN: 978-1-63980-185-5

Kelsay Books
502 South 1040 East, A-119
American Fork, Utah 84003
Kelsaybooks.com

"The human animal is a beast that dies and if he's got money he buys and buys and buys and I think the reason he buys everything he can buy is that in the back of his mind he has the crazy hope that one of his purchases will be life everlasting!—Which it never can be . . ."
—Tennessee Williams, *Cat on a Hot Tin Roof*

For Paige, Hayley and Mariel.
Because it's all about you.

Note from the Author

The definitions that can be seen at each section of this book come from my mother's dictionary, found in her desk, after her death. It is the *New Universal Self-Pronouncing Dictionary, with Encyclopedic Appendix.* Handy Edition. Based on the Foundation laid by Noah Webster. The John C. Winston Company, Philadelphia, Chicago, 1925. And the definitions are exceptional.

Dedication

To all those who join me in their search for meaning in odd objects inherited, abandoned and acquired.

A huge thank you with deep gratitude to Marie Kane's KT poetry group in Bucks County and to the fabulous Stalwart Poets, who help to add the words, cut the words, and discover new words.
I am especially indebted to the gifted and beloved late Dr. Chris Bursk. He is not only missed; he is irreplaceable.

To Jeanne Marie Beaumont and Estha Weiner—talented poets and teachers, generous with time and friendship—thank you, thank you.

A special thank you to Ken, for asking to read my poetry even when hesitant with his response. Safe and steady—always wise. You are my best fan—so happy to have you at my side.

Acknowledgments

A Certain Kind of Swagger: "New York, 1932"

After Happy Hour Review: "Polaroid," "Funny the Things We Recall"

Arsenic Lobster: "Gotcha"

Bucks County Anthology: "New Hope"

Covenant of the Generations: "The Nut Brown Sweater," "My Father's Arms"

Family by the Poet: "Polaroid"

Love and Ensuing Madness: "Marital Aids"

MacQueen's Quinterly, Issue 12: "Family Gathering"

Memsahib Memories: 'Copper Trays," "Lahore Gold," "My Paandaani"

Poetry Super Highway's 24th Annual Yom HaShoah Issue: "The Grand Prix Chromonica"

Schuylkill Journal Review: "Dandelion"

Silver Birch Press: "My Daughter Gave Me an Orchard," "Wild Raspberries"

Then and Now: "Grandma's Kitchen"

Contents

I. Things — 17

CRJ1972	19
A Rather Odd Souvenir	20
Containers	21
Dandelion	23
Last Will on Fentanyl	24
A Clutch of Eggs	26
The Forsaken Little Black Book	28
Copper Tray	30
The Nut Brown Sweater	31
My Daughter Bought Me an Orchid Plant	32
Salt and Pepper	34
The Presto Jar	35
Inga Stinkfinger	36
Her Mother Said It Was a Rattle	37
Maybe It Was Her Profile	38
The Glass Ibex	39
Dishes of the Dead	41
The Grand Prix Chromonica	43
Gotcha	44
Wild Raspberries	45

II. Places — 47

Evening in Paris	49
Glen Patrick's	50
June in Asia, 2009	51
Room in New York, 1932	53
My Paandani	54
Lahore Gold	55
Guilt on the Tow Path	56
New Hope	57
Conversation with a *Znicz*	58

Dog in an Empty Townhouse	59
Family Gathering	61
It's not Spring until	63

III. Memories   65

Memories	65
Demolition Derby	67
Funny the Things We Recall	68
Grandma's Kitchen	69
I Never Heard My Grandfather's Voice	71
Polaroid	72
December 15th and the Dragonflies Are Gone	73
Memory	74
The Future Is Fuchsia	75
Memory 2	77
Peace by Understanding	78
Memory 3	80
Hey Mom,	81
Dear Dad,	82

IV. Revelations   83

Tell Me a Story	85
Edna Sits on My Shoulder	86
Ode to an Incision	87
Dementia, a Pantoum	88
Lokshen Kugel	89
It Begins with a Delmonico	90
Hamsa	91
Everybody Loves Somebody Sometime	92
Marital Aids	94
Miracle Mike	95

My Father's Arms	96
It's a Shade	98
Lunatic	100

V. Conclusion 101

Who Are These People?	103
The Jewish Funeral	105
In Appreciation for Her Final Observation	106
The Shadow Knows	107
Silver Spoons	108
My Yizkor Moment	109
Born in Brooklyn	110

I
Things

thing: *whatever is distinct from intelligent beings; inanimate matter*

CRJ1972

Because I collected the quarters from the ashtray.
Because I removed the Betty Boop floor mats.
Because I placed the fishing rods from your trunk into my own.
Because I tossed the cushions, towels and that beaded seat cover.
Because I took two pairs of sunglasses and the auto wallet
that smelled of Nautica.
Because I found the Nautica.
Because I kept the crate that contained baby wipes, upholstery
cleaner, liquid lighter fluid, flashlight, first-aid kit, silly umbrella
hat and squeegee.
Because my hands assaulted your glove compartment, console
and seat pockets.
Because I unearthed your emergency flare and medical supplies
(all expired).
Because the Metallic Seattle Blue had only one dent after six
month's use.
Because I sat where you sat against the grey velour upholstered
seats.
Because it still had that new car scent you loved so.
Because I needed to touch everything your hands had touched.
Because I stood in line at the 34th Street DMV.
Because I clutched the plates to my chest and memorized them.
Because I had to sell your car.
Because I thought you would vanish from my thoughts.
Because then, and only then, I learned it doesn't work that way.

A Rather Odd Souvenir

The Japanese champlevé vase bought in China
around 1920, give or take, on a honeymoon.
Carted back to East Flatbush and like the couple,
a little out of place.
Bronze. Lots of champlevé enamel. Handles
ornately swirled from the top to its broad hips.
Lotus flowers and deco shapes formed a lovely
border, but the bulging center was what caught
your eye. Deep green scales curled the width
of each side. Scarlet fire came from a dragon's
nose and two branched horns topped its head.
White smoke sat on his bottom lip and a fine
yellow line alluded to a reptile belly
which the couple followed, as if they were held
captive by a forked tail.

Containers

Trash does not pretend to be anything better than it is
—Wislawa Szymborska

Jones Beach sand in an old Presto jar
with a small oyster shell on top,
grains collected before leaving Long Island.

The large Persian copper bowl
overflowing with nautilus, conch, cockle,
tulip banded, sand dollar, snail
and many, many wentletraps.

And the rocks I carried home
to be stored in specific containers
as their final resting place.
There is nothing arbitrary about the selection:

two jagged pieces of slate from Millay's Steepletop
taken from under the Do Not Trespass sign before her house
and stored in a glass bowl beside a brass pandaani
that holds two more rocks from the Masada cliffs
and a thousand secrets that need to be known.

Grand Canyon sedimentary rock,
the lines of separation of thousands of years
and the colors of sunset watched from the North Rim.

In my bedroom are the rocks from Auschwitz.
Specifically Block 10—Aunt Ray's home
for more than three years. Not that she spoke of it.
These are stored in a bronze jar
and though they are rarely caressed,
I know they are always right beside me.

And I have my aunt's buttons too.
Not just the ones I hand-sewed to cover the body
of my voodoo doll Esta,
but the ones stored in a small hand-painted box
with three drawers,
all the old metal, plastic, and glass buttons
Ray had stored everywhere
in her Coney Island apartment
on Surf Avenue, across from the aquarium,
buttons in a large plastic tooth,
in covered soap dishes, in Ziploc bags,
I took them all.
Some call this trash, but is it?
When you hold a shell, rock or button,
when you really take your time,
each one has a story.
A few even scream.

Dandelion

wrapped in faded folded
wax paper and discovered
in the top drawer
of her mother's armoire,
she became that five-year-old girl
first plucking them from the grass
then running into the kitchen
look what I picked for you.
Into a Flintstone jelly glass
they would go,
but they never lasted long.
They never rivaled
the large sunflowers
that graced the dining room table.
She thought her mother's smile
obligatory, unimpressed.
But she found this pressed dead
dandelion, after all these years,
and then recalled
how they would pick the weed
when it was a fuzzy white ball,
lean in together, head-to-head,
and make a silent wish,
don't tell—just blow.

Last Will on Fentanyl

a Ghazal

I found the list on a legal pad, my father's script, labeled "ICOD"
(in case of death), when I emptied my mother's desk—
not as planned.

Silver spoon collection: "Who will polish them when I'm gone?"
"Not me Dad." Got them anyway, just as he planned.

Grandma's curio to a cousin: No. She didn't bother to attend the
funeral. And I don't ship. So much for best laid plans.

Pewter Victorian woman's bust: I tossed in a donation box but my
daughter brought it back. Now sits on Dickinson's poems—
an accidental plan.

Large Lladro horses on a stand, you specifically said go to Brian.
We never figured out why—was this all you had planned?

Brass bird cage with distorted porcelain parrots: Seriously, who
wants this? Natalie: "They remind me of family." Funny plan.

Churchill/FDR Fight for Democracy plate: that's mine!
Ellis Island historic souvenir, for grandchildren—a future plan.

Bronze chandelier with sawed off swastikas to nephew: Nope.
This goes to the boy who wanted your stolen Nazi sword—
my plan.

DW Haddon oil on wood board painting to Ron or Julie: for forty
years you swore this had value. Christies disagreed.
Now what's the plan?

Two more curios gifted to me: porcelain shoes, dogs and cats,
which you knew I detested. Funny on Fentanyl plan.

I kept your expert carving knives and the *Chef's Choice* sharpener.
We all wanted these, but they'll just have to wait
and that's a good plan.

For the record: Brian knew exactly where you stashed the gun,
you know—with oak stand and engraved plate that read,
Last Resort—pivotal plan.

A Clutch of Eggs

Here's what I know:
She kept it enclosed in a glass dome
that fit over a brass plate with fake red velvet,
peeling, by the time it became mine.

Here's what I remember:
She told me it belonged to her mother.
And despite their loud arguments, door slams,
and Sunday dinners cut short,

she treasured her and this piece. Which became
my piece. So the first course of action?
Toss the dome.
I hate fake, peeling red velvet.

A porcelain girl stands in a clump of trees,
small, impish, fine lines marking
her eyes and lips,
undoubtedly the ugliest piece either woman owned.

She holds a nosegay of flowers in one hand,
woven basket at her feet. And inside that?
A clutch of eggs.
No hen, duck or robin.

My memories were of an angry mother,
because this piece was all she got.
And she wanted more.
Nothing ever seemed enough.

It took me years to figure out it had nothing
to do with 'the stuff.' It was neglect.
Growing up poor. Fights with her mother.
Fighting for attention. A smile. A nod.

I think this ugly piece might be rare. Valuable.
I know it's fragile because two of the branches
are chipped, one by her,
the other by me.

Should have kept the dome.

The Forsaken Little Black Book

Wedged in the back of her lady's desk,
well-worn leather cover held together
by three small pieces of Scotch tape:

>New Universal
>Self-Pronouncing
>Dictionary
>Handy Edition

Three signatures on the inside front page,
my mother's name listed last,
the first name dated Jan. 6, 1926.

>lady: *a well-bred woman*
>desk: *a pulpit*

Three fragile pieces of Scotch tape
bound this book throughout my mother's life.

>tape: *a narrow band of linen*
>life: *existence; spirit*

The pages, past yellow, flaking apart,
and yet, this six-inch edition contained
all the knowledge she ever needed:

>Business Terms by Murray Gross
>Measure Units and Chemical Elements
>Forms of Address used in Ceremonious Communications
>with persons of Title or Official Position
>and The Jewish Calendar
>located directly above the Zodiac

Not an underline. Not one page dog-eared,
or pen marked.
Next to her signature, no date but *LB#63*,
the local draft board, in Jamaica, Queens.
No doubt stored in the top drawer of her gray metal desk

> draft: *detachment of soldiers; amount drunk*
> doubt: *uncertainty of mind*

Almost every book that entered our front door,
this woman tossed out, but not this one.
This one seemed sacred, and it held the key
to her quirky expressions.

> dear: *expensive, costly*
> nubbin: *an imperfect ear of corn*

Published before she was born,
perhaps gifted by her mother,
who gave little, especially of herself,
making this book a salve for a hurt soul.

> mother: *the female superior of a religious house*
> guilt: *crime; sin*

She likely forgot she shoved this book
on the back shelf of her lady's desk
because she would have grabbed it,
to secure the words, stop them from flight.
But she couldn't, so they left
and she had no way to get them back.
Like these pages, they crumbled
and softly slipped away.
Despite three deliberate pieces of Scotch tape.

Copper Tray

Found in the heat of Anarkahli Bazaar, half-hidden on the back
shelf of a cluttered copper stall in Lahore. Its owner pretended
resistance. How could he possibly part with his favorite tray?

Or was it you? Did he simply want you to stay? Your dark eyes,
shiny brown hair, like the women of his country, but not.
You bartered well, shared a smile, a handshake and as he pocketed

rupees you collected the tray. Remember how you hoped for a hot
shower when you got home? Soot flowed from hair, grime slid
from your hands as you steamed the bath and washed off

Lahore. Remember that first party at Main Colony? Spent two days
cooking and arranging. Pounded, then marinated undercut,
expecting it miraculously turned tender. You wore a flowing wrap

skirt and patent red sandals. The new tray shone bright. Filled
with stemware and home-made wine that Sharif offered to guests.
Sharif, sweet, but so nervous, as glassware rattled, wine splattered,

until you freed him of the tray and sent him back to the kitchen.
Relieved. Both of you. That was long ago. So far away. Today
you find yourself in Macy's—to shop for business clothes

for your daughter. Took that old oak escalator up to five. Watched
as a different girl posed in the mirror, but saw your reflection
look back. Twice. The shiny, bright copper tray faces.

It was like a splendid dream suddenly turned tart.
Wake up, my sweet—fly away! Return to Anarkhali bazaar
once more. Water buffalo and tongas, Urdu and hand motions.

Dust storms, intense heat. Women shrouded in black holding one
child's hand, balancing another on her hip when suddenly
a tall dark American girl with long lean legs runs by.

The Nut Brown Sweater

Mamaleh, they took my things away from me.
May nineteen forty-two—my hair was long
and thick dark brown with waves that they quickly
cut all off. I was in my favorite nut brown
sweater jacket. They let me wear that as
I boarded the long black train to Auschwitz.

My mother, Cutla, came from Warsaw as
did my father, Herman. They put them on
a train that went to the crematorium—
there were so many I never knew which one.
And the children—we saw them board. We knew.
We knew then we would never see them again.

The number on my left arm? 13088.
You need a witness mister? I have none.
I have nobody. I am the only one alive
from the whole transport. No one else.
I went to Brooklyn, USA. Me and
My Abey. We married in Bergen-Belsen

then came here in 'forty-nine as tailors.
I was in my nut-brown sweater jacket
and kept it with me 'til the day I died.
Julaleh, your hands go through all my things,
yet will they stop at this old brown sweater?
I'm here, your guiding hand, do not overlook.

Good, you see and cradle it in your arms.
You set it aside, not knowing why.
And then you find the framed photograph—
of me in the same sweater with my long, lovely hair.
We knew then we were alone together.

My Daughter Bought Me an Orchid Plant

for Mother's Day
four years ago,
two days after
my mother died.

As a rule,
I kill orchids,
which my mother
had often said I did
to her.

I was not one
to be generous
with water,
somehow,
despite me,
this orchid survived.

It thrived,
grew more leaves
even rose again,
pale pink flowers
on twin stems,
as if it had a will
to stay alive.

This winter
has been long
and stagnant.
The orchid
has endured,
has grown
two sturdy sprouts.
I am still waiting.

Like a resurrection
of sorts,
this Mother's Day
plant. Or is it
my mother's hand,
somehow rising
from a grave,
to promise,
this one will live.

Salt and Pepper

Green depression glass
placed next to my stove
more than forty years ago.
My mother found them
at a flea market in Shohola.

My father, a kid and in the army,
had a nickname: Pepper.
All his letters to his love
ended with a simple line sketch:
a shaker and a single letter: P

When my mother was in the ER
and the nurses surrounded,
she smiled at me and sang:
salt and pepper, salt and pepper.

As if my dad was in the house.
As if to tell me she was the salt
because I never figured that out.
As if the calm that enveloped me
was not a coincidence.

And when she died twelve hours
later, the song my father sang
to me, as a kid, played on the radio:
Mares eat oats;
Does eat oats;
Little lambs eat ivy . . .

Pepper with Salt.

The Presto Jar

It holds about a cup of smooth beach sand. This vintage glass Presto jar, its closure approved by the Good Housekeeping Institute. Beige, white, black grains that sparkle in light. Sand from Long Island's south shore. Sand first captured by the presto jar, then screwed in place by the glass plate, followed by the metal lid, and finally turned tightly until it could not be turned at all. She smiles when she holds it, the weight of it feeling right, collected from Jones Beach, the same beach the family went to long ago.

She remembered a wagon pulling her and a large red metal cooler, with Coca Cola written in white script. They went through the tunnel from Parking Field 4 to get to the boardwalk. A damp tunnel that felt like forever until they could spread their blanket across the hot sand. It took her to a day, a breeze that once blew against her mother's black curls while her father chased her kicking up sand with every step, laughing as they sank into it.

She recalled the feel of it between her fingers and toes, and the memory of burying her father, diligently patting, shoveling, giggling, until he was covered to his neck, until he freed his hands for an unfiltered Chesterfield.

She smiles, turns the jar upside down, considers the slight shift of sand and fantasized that these were indeed the same grains from that day. The day she first buried her father.

Inga Stinkfinger

He told the child that was its name,
and the girl looked up at him
with enormous disappointment.

It was a far cry from what she wanted,
plus it smelled, a musty, molded-plastic
odor that permeated.

Inga was a first edition troll doll,
another Dam doll from Denmark,
a '60s thing. The original troll.

The child didn't care—wanted a baby doll,
cuddly and soft with pink, rosy cheeks,
pouty mouth, maybe a touch of blonde hair.

This doll, not only stunk; she was truly ugly,
all seven inches of her, with that wild
black untamed hair

in pig tails tied with green felt fabric
that matched her skirt, and suspenders,
which fell over a yellow shirt.

The eyes were bulging and brown with laugh
wrinkles that melted into deep lines which
surrounded a broad smile and puffed out cheeks.

Her feet were supported by squat, thick, moveable
legs, the hands large with fingers outspread
all four of them, to match the four fat toes.

The gifter looked hard at his daughter:
no one wanted to take her since she is so ugly,
but I knew you would love her in spite of that.

Her Mother Said It Was a Rattle

Her mother said it was her rattle
and there was no reason
for doubt.
But fingering it now,
this small brass bell,
once wholly painted,
now only a blotch of green
and white remain.
Hung on a red leather strap
with a fuzzy strand
of wool fringe
in several earth tones.
No pink. No blue.

Her mother said it was her rattle
and the girl took
her at her word.
No question. No doubt.
But it looked more like a cat bell.
Did it belong to Buster?

And was this the best
they could do?
After all, she was the second daughter.

Maybe It Was Her Profile

since her nose was similar to mine.
Or maybe it was her almond eyes,
but I don't think that's likely.
Her hair was piled
high on her head,
in a loose bun
trimmed with rosebuds
and pearls.
So it was definitely not that.
It wasn't the high collar
or puffed sleeves,
I'm sure.
Maybe it was because this bust
of a Victorian woman
in solid pewter
without any signature
on the bottom
was just something
my father knew I wouldn't
like or want. Just maybe he had
no idea who else to give
her to. Or maybe it made
him think of me.
Maybe it was his favorite thing.

The Glass Ibex

Ray, I want you to give her the Ibex when I'm gone.
She dismissed him with a swift wave of her arm.
Do you hear me? I want to make sure she gets it.

Her uncle was blanketed in the multi-colored granny-stitch
afghan that her aunt made for him. Stage 4 lung cancer.
This man who survived Dachau and Auschwitz would not
survive the cigarettes he smoked all day at the shirt factory.

Now this Ibex was more than a conversation piece. It was half
the height of his niece and solid lead glass. Huge orange ribbed
glass curled out of its head to a sharp point. Cool to the touch
and fun to run your hands along, the girl still hated it.

Perhaps the horns frightened her, or the burden of ownership
felt heavier than those ornate orange horns.
She did not want it. And years later, when both uncle and aunt
were dead, the girl now grown, still looked at the Ibex and said,
No!

She called the Russian movers to take most of the furniture.
A neighbor came to take whatever else was left—stopped
and asked about the Ibex. The girl looked again and said, *No!*

She could hear his voice, his heavy Polish accent. She warmed
at the memory of his smile, Chesterfield held between fingers
on his right hand, numbers tattooed in dark blue on the left.

The Ibex had no eyes, but she looked deep into their indented
space and it became a mirror. A mirror that reflected the image
of her uncle—at his best—healthy, sitting on the edge of his bed,
yelling at the TV, a Yankee game: *No! No!—play right.*
And she found comfort there.

She grabbed two king-sized pillowcases, bagged the Ibex and took him home.

Dishes of the Dead

line the shelves of my kitchen cabinets,
emerging on holidays to take center
stage on the table, reminding me
of a time when there wasn't so much
extra space between the plates.

The lidded gold-speckled casserole belonged
to my aunt who brought it to our house
every Thanksgiving filled with sweet
potatoes and golden marshmallows.

The sterling shot glass, which was my father's
Bar Mitzvah Kiddush cup always holds
Manischewitz and has his initials, 'HT' engraved
on one side, the Star of David on the other.

The Corningware with its' signature blue
cornflower belonged to my mother.
She filled it with that old faithful string bean
recipe using Campbell's Cream of Mushroom
and topped it off with Durkee fried onions.

Dessert cups were my mother-in-law's
hobnail champagne glasses, which
held fruit cocktail, some fresh,
some canned. And the centerpiece
was always my grandmother's vase,

cut glass, not crystal, with two handles
and a chip that only I could find.
Still striking when filled with sunflowers
and hydrangeas, taking center stage on the table.

We never thought about these dishes
as they went to and fro one home
to the other. We just knew that they would,
and for years they did.

When I sleep I dream not just about
these people, but their special cuisine,
the manner they served. I see their old
kitchens, I sit down beside them.
But the dishes always remain empty.

The Grand Prix Chromonica

Supershiny chrome, impressive for its years,
and trimmed in dark burl wood—Aunt Ray's
German made M. Hohner harmonica.
Like so many of her proud possessions,
she stoutly believed German goods
were the only way to go. Replacements
for what was ravaged from this Warsaw woman.

Now the other items, like her cherished Eberthal china
or Fisher stereo console made sense,
(would have been a German car if either of them drove),
But a harmonica—one that could possibly pre-date WWII
and commemorated the Grand Prix races Hohner won?

Did Ray or Abe play harmonica? Not likely. And like them,
how did this particular treasure survive Auschwitz?

Gotcha

1.
So—
My children
decide to marry
my husband plans retirement
I'm pushed to leave New York
So—
I reach out to the dead.
What do I do?
I begin to sew.

2.
Esta, muslin doll, color of Coney Island,
blue, red, crystal, beige and gold,
covered in buttons carefully chosen,
by hands that once held my own.

When shaken these buttons knock together
like teaspoons against glass cups,
perfect round breasts are red and gold,
the one on her head? fabric fluff.

Two bold beige buttons clasp her buttocks,
she has power to summon the dead.
A pox on them! cries Grandma Leah,
tell me my mamaleh, she said.

3.
When I hold her she penetrates my palm.
On her own she takes flight,
across the room, from chair to chair,
to her throne with that indigo stare.

If necessary she will take you out.
Es ken gemolt zein.

Wild Raspberries

a Duplex

On a bad news day we picked wild raspberries.
They were tart, but not distasteful—a little like us.

> The jelly rings went sour and left a lingering taste.
> Three deaths, one hastened, one forlorn, one unborn.

Three lives hastened, unborn, forlorn, have left their mark.
She could not recall which leg had the smooth, oval, snake bite.

> Lilith's bite is worse than a snake's and leaves a smooth oval stain.
> The old woman believed every death was merely an end of story.

Do not end the story on an old woman's belief.
The goal is to ingest every word in every book he wrote.

> Every book, every word he wrote is a most worthy goal.
> The deep ache is a reminder to keep breathing.
> Keep breathing.

Keep breathing. Despite the deep ache. Keep breathing.
We picked wild raspberries on a day full of bad news.

II
Places

place: *special locality; residence; passage in a book*

Evening in Paris

was never a night on the town,
or romantic fantasy,
but a 2 oz. blue glass bottle
of cologne by Bourjois.

The scent that reminded me
of my mother. Not that I ever
recall her wearing it.
But I do remember

where it was kept: a brass
mirrored tray atop a kidney
shaped vanity, with a floor length
curtain where I would hide.

And when no one was around
I would uncap the plastic pointed
silver top, put my finger
over the opening and tip,

then dab behind my ears
before I deeply inhaled the too sweet
smell of my mother,
who probably never wore it.

Glen Patrick's

once famous as McNulty's in Ozone Park, was the gin
mill where Kerouac, Cassady and Ginsberg drank
and wrote, but more, it was my dad's bar. The bar
that called him Harry, at the corner of Crossbay and Linden.

Sometimes I joined him there—to escape my mother's
scrutiny and appreciate the familiar scent of stale booze
that stained heavily shellacked old wood—the kind that dared
you to slide your drink straight down as far as it would go.

Vinnie, a retired cop, sat in the same seat next
to the door every day. He sat sideways, his view
of the street never completely blocked. Mary ran the place
and had heard all about my mother *and* my father's woes.
It's a bar—everybody has a story.

When my father died I took the family to toast
the man we called Harold. Vinnie kissed me hello.
I exhaled deeply, ordered vodka straight up. The family—
they seemed in shock. They scorned the Libby barware,
the blue-collar vibe and couldn't exit quick enough.

But I felt at home, seated on Kerouac's stool.
the one right next to my dad's.
The ghosts here are superb.

June in Asia, 2009

I

The torii looked like a house of mirrors to the Shinto
entry, and it is all about the ascent. One after another,
vermillion gates designed to deliver. To open the mind,
heart and eyes. To journey through each gate until ancestors
become within reach, protection from evil, a kaleidoscope
to the afterlife, before the downward return to the mundane.

Orange wood
torii, lanterns and stone
beads for sale

II

Shopping in Seoul's people packed streets, giggling girls,
tourists and souvenirs that ranged from tacky toys to lacquer,
mother of pearl, silk blouses, Celadon ceramics and Asian
art. And lots of jade: yellow, light and dark green, pendants
carved with cranes to signify longevity, eternity even,
but still, doesn't ease the pain of recent death.

Insadong
walk for wedding ducks
soundless stroll

III

Dongdaemun fabric market was reminiscent of old New York's
garment center, but the bolts and buttons looked and smelled
different. Dongdaemun, packed with satin silks, lined
longing, crowded with hunger. Burgundy and evergreen
embroidered cushions line luggage for the return home.

Silk cushions
a sweet hidden teahouse
Flex your toes

IV

Sofitel Hotel in Seoul had four restaurants to choose: Chinese,
Japanese, a coffee shop, and western steaks cowboy style.
But the bar was the only late-night option. Cheese plates, fruit
and vodka tonics until they closed. Four very young women sang
70's tunes to the last hour.
His funeral held a week ago.

Filipino
girls serenade the bar
We toast death

V

The cap that belonged to Harry (not his real name
but the name the bartender gave him) left by the base
of the metal stool. Coffee brown, satin lining. His favorite.
He drank vodka and cranberry juice so his wife wouldn't know.
Glen Patrick's Bar. Kerouac's place. Ginsberg hung there too.

Corduroy
hat sits on my chair
smelling of you

Room in New York, 1932

Edward Hopper painting

To live in a brownstone in Washington Square
with that handsome man, the shock of white
of his shirt, the shadows that outline strong shoulders,
muscular arms. The black tie tucked in by collar
and vest. And your window, uncurtained, wide open.

But the walls of this brownstone—where are the shelves
lined by books, ceiling to floor, the musty smell
of leather, paper, fresh ink—permanence?
To live in a brownstone in Washington Square,
there must be books.

Seems to this voyeur, more than that oak table
separates the two of you.
Landscape prints make this room even darker, your dress,
the tufted club chair and a lampshade the sole source of light.
And you—side saddled on the piano bench,

head bent down, in your lovely red sleeveless frock,
a subtle hint of ruffle at your back, as your index finger
lightly strokes a random key. What song plays in your head?
Alone Together or Willow Weep for Me?
And yet, his eyes are devoted to news in the evening *Sun*.

Did you spend time at *Chumley's* earlier this eve?
It's been said that sometimes Millay mans the bar—
she's a so-so listener, but keen to spout a sonnet request:
I would indeed that love were longer-lived . . . she has said.

Oh that door! It looms perfectly centered between
the two of you. And you, still seated on the piano bench,
still not committed to that seat. That door beckons,
the window tempts, you can hear music from the street,
and the night still so young, why linger any longer?

My Paandani

Pretty old, fully functional although not in use.
Octagonal copper container, floral embossed
with a working clip. The lid's metal handle
no longer holds.
Purchased from a metal stall in Raja Bazaar.
An antique . . . no, museum piece.
Weren't they all? Well, it was well-
bartered to be sure. Tray still covers six metal
compartments colored by tobacco, cardamom,
cloves. Lethal breath mints wrapped in betel
leaves that were once sold then spit
staining every street. For thirty years
it held tissues that casket teeth—baby teeth
puppy molars. Stick-figure drawings. Notes.
Take my tooth and give me money.
Fairly forgotten on a credenza in the den.
Rotted teeth. Jagged little bones.
Character wears better on copper.
My paandani. Punjabi palate cleanser kit.

Lahore Gold

I travelled to Lahore:
Pakistan's district for gems,
adorned with fast tongas,
amid sluggish buffalo.

Purdah'd women
prepared to shove
and I was prepared
to shove right back.

Arrived at Afzal's
and happily rolled
two bangles onto my wrist
when she grabbed me.

Shrouded in black polyester
waving her finger, 'no.'
(Now I regretted not
wearing my scarf.)

She slipped a third
bangle on and as our eyes
met, we smiled.
Ah, gold.

Guilt on the Tow Path

A dining needle accompanied me
mid-morning on the tow path.
I hadn't seen one since I was a kid,
and this one flitted between my every step.

Its presence around my ankles awakened
another memory of the white butterfly
in my driveway years ago, my pigtails
flying, my feet jumping rope. The butterfly

became entangled, one wing stolen
by rope, so I purposely crushed it,
pretended it was no big deal—
an ordinary butterfly—not a monarch.

Good thing my dragonfly is unaware
of that cruelty because it remains
by my feet—sticking with my stride.
Too bad it can't tell me which tree cradles

a fledgling eagle and its leaf-veiled nest.
My thoughts wander yet again—to my son,
as a toddler, we were young, house poor,
somewhat stuck, I struck him.

But the slap was harder than intended.
An accident. I knew I was negligent.
An annoying memory that won't disappear.
The dining needle still lingers, still unharmed.

We find the fledgling, perched on its nest rim,
stoic, perhaps righteous, but quite alone.
Not yet ready for flight, more likely
watching for mother and trusting its world.

New Hope

To go to Bucks County, to your daughter's wedding, to book
the most charming inn on the farm, where all the food is grown,
and they have a goat.

To know this womanchild of yours desires simplicity and respect,
to keep your thoughts to yourself, bite your lip 'til it bleeds,
shake a voodoo doll.

To visit the inn and ogle old photos from 1938, George S.
Kaufman, Lillian Hellman, Harpo Marx. To learn once
it was Kaufman's home. They played tennis, sat by the pool.

To write screenplays and Broadway shows that got produced.
To return to the wedding planning.

To acknowledge that some of these bridal shops
display dresses that display a lot of skin (a lot) and look
like something you would see in Brighton Beach or Israel.

To learn that the Hammersteins are still involved with the
Playhouse, to read Michener and Pearl S. Buck
because they all lived here too.

To not be pissed because your daughter rejects every blessed idea
you present, to not tell her you're going to put lavender stress
cream in the hospitality bags because they come from Peace Valley
and to not care that she does not like lavender.
It's stress cream for Christ's sake.

To step aside because this is her time, you had yours. She danced
in red and gold feathers to Hello Dolly,
she'll dance in lace and flowered garland hair.

Conversation with a *Znicz*

(znicz are the memorial candles used in Poland's cemeteries)
after Wislawa Szymborska's "Conversation with a Stone"

I know, there are always a number
of you there, especially around
her birthday or deathday, and I guess
not all might be for her, since
her ashes rest with her parents and sister.
But pretty certain most of you are.
And most of you are red, some white,
and while the amber ones are lovely,
I would select blue. It suits her best.

What are my thoughts, you ask?
I seem to have a lot of regret. No, not just
regret I never met her. I feel like
we had Poland in common. No, not poetry.
My words pale next to hers. Regret,
not envy mind you, I believe
my regret has more to do with denial.
Not Wislawa. Absolutely not her.

Regret arrives with ease when you stand
on Poland's soil. Especially here,
at Rakowicki Cemetery. At least she knows
where she is and it's not alone. Krakow earth.
My family? They remain in Warsaw, not far
from here. I don't know where, but they have
lots of company, all nameless. Now I regret
I don't know who they were. Or how many.
Or what they looked like.

I am glad her grave suits her. A simple grave.
Definitely a blue *znicz* is in order. So much nicer
than the *yahrzeit* candles my people use.
I must remember to bring a match.

Dog in an Empty Townhouse

> response to Wislawa Szymborska's "Cat in an Empty Apartment"

Cats are survivors—
Dogs, on the other hand, are extremely limited:
loyal, and loving, they really can't be left behind,
can't climb the walls like a cat, but do pace
up and down, down and up, always waiting,
waiting by the front door
waiting by the food bowl.
A dog is helpless. And will wait.

Of course, we all know your poem was not
about the cat. And it does make me think
of love and being left behind,
alone in the dark,
listening to sounds outside
a bolted door.
That feeling you get when the clock
is silent and you can feel time stop.

Someone was always here, and also there,
and then they were not.
The dog doesn't get it
but I think I do.
I have gone through those closets,
shelves, and never missed a drawer.

It doesn't get more personal.
All those random items, coded notes, cards,
trinkets—never saw that ring before.
Not meant for someone else's eyes to see
or hands to touch. Another violation.
Even privacy dies.

The dog has no clue his master won't return.
Cannot understand why.
And I'm not all that sure we do either.
We always think there will be time,
the battery will not die, so no need to explain
a stained shirt, a note kept
in the bottom drawer
with a photo of someone else
that perhaps you knew but didn't know.
Sometimes, just sometimes, the dog is the lucky one.

Family Gathering

Arbeit macht frei
not quite a welcome sign,
but it led me to the ovens.
Took my breath away,
that air we shared.

Flesh, hair, bones.

*They took the Kinder,
on the trains they went,
and we knew
we knew
we knew we would never
see them again.*

Bones, hair, flesh

My grandmother's family,
all except two,
whole villages,
some never had time for their tattoo,
straight to the ovens.

Hair, bones, flesh

The metal door taunted,
beckoned, threatened.
I could smell their ashes.
I saw exactly how
they were pushed
to one side
to allow for more.

Bones, flesh, hair

How many?
Did we look alike?
Think alike?

I stood
where they stood.

It's not Spring until

you inhale the damp soil after a heavy
rain, the daffodils and hyacinths dig out
and the forsythia by my bedroom sprouts

yellow. But can it compare with the run
to Joe's Candy Store when I was ten?
Not if he just stocked the shelves

with brand-new Spalding high bounce balls
and Duncan Imperial yo-yos. And if your
personal preference was ruby red—you best

be quick. I loved the smell of the fresh
rubber, but it wore off as quick as the blue
script when you bounced it a few times.

Now the yoyo never wore me down.
You just had to master the quick flick
of your wrist and learn how to yank up

fast before it completely unwound.
I never did get past just making it go
up and down, up and down. Rewind.

But when my father walked through
our kitchen door, I couldn't wait
to stretch out my hand to place that yoyo

into his. I watched as he wound the cord,
his wrist powerful and practiced,
followed by a few fast furious throws.

He *walked the dog* and *rocked the baby*.

III
Memories

memory: *that faculty of the mind by which it retains the knowledge of previous occurrences and thoughts*

Demolition Derby

My father loved them.
Would take me, my brother
and my mother's mother
to the rink in West Hempstead
marked by the 1964 World's Fair
arch for *Peace by Understanding*.
(At least the arch remains.)

But it was the roller derby
that I loved the most.
Tiny would feign injury,
then take off like a bat
out of hell. Wheels
on her skates smokin' dust.

The rest of her team,
Tequila Sheila, Infernal Myrtle,
Nutcracker and Big Red,
were good enough. But Tiny,
arms clenched to chest,
padded knees slightly bent,
speedily passed them all.

Wonder what became of her.
Wonder if she ever wore black
stiletto heels, or perhaps
got all gussied up, spritzer
in hand and ever ready
to dance a flawless tango?

I sure hope not.

Funny the Things We Recall

My cousins, a random red-faced cantor and a couple of Persian
in-laws buried my aunt on Sunday. Lowered in the ground,
next to my uncle, almost five years to the day he died.
Her son covered her casket, one shovel of mustard brown dirt
at a time, making sure this woman who didn't believe, was buried
the proper Kosher way. He and the red-faced cantor took shovel
after shovel after shovel until the dirt was gone. And when
his sister's knees buckled he stopped, steadied her, then picked up
the shovel to carry on.

It was nine degrees. I could no longer feel my toes, stood stiffly
silent, watching them shovel and struggle.
And then I was at the beach, Jones Beach. Four years old,
sitting next to a red metal cooler with Coca-Cola written
in thick white script. I wore a navy cardigan (because my mother
kept me in sweaters—no matter how hot), but my cousins
were bare chested and blonde with matching shovel and pails
covered in beach balls, star fish and sand.
Mustard brown sand.

Grandma's Kitchen

I discovered Leah when I was nine.
She sat one row behind
at my brother's Bar Mitzvah.
Who's that funny looking lady?
Your grandma. My mom.

Her Brighton Beach apartment was her pride:
thick metal bar that locked floor to door,
plaster cast foot with geraniums on top,
painted murals on china cabinets
containing German and Italian knockoffs.

But she was from Warsaw;
before the war,
before the others saw.

Mostly I remember her kitchen—
one large window overlooking rooftops,
elevated subways, which rattled Venetian
blinds every time the B whipped by.

White wallpaper that looked like bricks
with green ivy crawling—directing—
my eyes to the kitchen's corner,
to the mannequin that stood alone.

Short and squat like Leah. Same broad
bust, waist, hips. Headless. Legless too.
A skirt or shirt always pinned in place.
Leah, proud card member of *ILGWU.

Once she measured me for a wool jumper.
Tape, pins, fabric and her hands all over me.
Mannequin must have served as my model—
that jumper was as big as my disappointment.

Nothing legal about her, declared my mom.
Perhaps it was the bathtub gin,
or card games with Dutch Schultz.
Maybe the pajamas, umbrellas and blouses
sold direct from her closet.

But I miss this woman I never got to know.
I miss the smell of simmering soup,
the flash from her gold facet earrings,
and her hands that held her hips, that held off
the old men who called her name.

I miss sitting with Dad at her table.

[*International Ladies Garment Workers' Union]

I Never Heard My Grandfather's Voice

My favorite photo had him standing on Coney Island
sand, alongside my grandmother, Nellie, in her bathing
costume, and he, leaning in towards her
in his three-piece suit, tie still in place.
But she left him, after the Depression. Took the girls
and went to California, to her parents,
and their quite comfortable Bellaire home.
Nat stayed in Brooklyn. No one ever said where.
Perhaps he kept this other photo I own on his dresser:
two young girls dressed in hand-me-down plaids,
four scraggly arms hugging a sycamore tree.
He must have missed most of their teen-age years,
even when they returned to Brooklyn (he was not to be seen,
said their mother). So he missed the bobby-socked,
saddle-shoed feet dangling off the fire escape,
where scarves were knit for soldiers. Missed their complaints
about Gregg shorthand and all those boorish boys
that taunted them at Tilden High. He missed taking them
to Nedicks for a Shatzkin knish, or Lundy's on the water for
steamers and clam chowder. No bumper cars. No Wonderwheel—
his girls were gone.
He lost his money, his home, and thanks to a tumor,
part of his mind.
Nathan, I wish I knew you beyond a photograph, or my mother's
tears and protests of love. For years I imagined your soft voice—
it had to be soft—the other voices were always so harsh.

Did I sit on your lap? Feel your arms surround me?
I would never have let you go.

Polaroid

They posed in size order, barefoot by the bundt cake:
my family at Thanksgiving—not one smile in the room.
Two held dish towels, Leah's legs wrapped in bandages.

Floral print aprons, ivy, brick and striped walls—the bandages
the only solid in this high-ceilinged kitchen. A chocolate cake
displayed like a trophy on a glass pedestaled plate centered
the room.

Union City, New Jersey, 1971: men smoking Chesterfields in the
living room, women drinking pina coladas from teacups.
Even Leah's bandages could not sway how they savored
the rum, devoured the home-made cake.

Cake, cigarettes, pina coladas—all in one room—
their love bandaged and preserved.

December 15th and the Dragonflies Are Gone

This bug has many names,
but I grew up knowing only one.
I've tried on a few of the others,
but they just don't seem to fit.
Not fond of mosquito fly or mosquito hawk.
Skeeter hawk? Don't like hawk at all.
Some say snake doctor, snake feeder,
or spindle. Spindle must have led to darner,
hence the darning needle.

But my mom, and not her alone, called it
the dining needle.
Apparently a bit of Brooklynese—
seems Brooklyn morphed darning to dining.
(Oh Lavinia, it does not need to make sense.)
And while I'm at it, happy birthday today
to my Brooklyn born and bred Mom.

Yes, we had a stoop.
Drank soda (too much).
And we called it a *Dining Needle*.
No matter where we went. And forevermore.

Memory

We were lunching
at Sarabeth's
on a spring day
my daughter,
in her twenties,
myself, far from it.
The waiter came
to take our order.

He never looked
my way,
but took the other order
most attentively.
Brought us our
wine and salad,
still not seeing me.

Until it was time
for the check,
then he looked
at me, no smile,
but he ever so gently
slipped me
the black plastic tray
with one mint.

The Future Is Fuchsia

I

That was the name
of the nail polish
my four-year-old
selected for her toes.

*I hope you can do this,
because the lady
at the salon
kept getting it
on my skin.*

My preference
for my short, split
nails would be
Topless and Barefoot
or Wild Nude,
but perhaps the color
Check in to Check out
is more apropos.

Oh Nana, you do this so well.
Finally—approval
and who doesn't crave that?
Maybe the time has come
for Smokin' hot
or Nightdreamer?
Probably too late,
better stick with my usual,
Tanascious Spirit.

II

Fire and Ice was what I wore
when Brian was a toddler of two.
He would sit with me at the kitchen
table, hands outstretched, *paint me*.

Until an hour before his dad
came home: I would feed the dog,
start dinner, remove Revlon red.
Boys don't wear polish, said Dad—
(unless it's Lincoln Park After Dark!)

Fire and Ice was a long time
resident in our house.
My daughter kept applying
and spilling it onto the same
old maple kitchen table
my grandmother picked up
from Salvation Army.

Nellie's nails were coated
in Lady Esther's colors: Flame,
Flesh, Lucky Rose.
It was simpler, less pressure,
no need to be clever.
How different do you think.
Scarlet or Jungle Rose
is from Muchi Muchi or Suits your Swell?

Memory 2

She stood next to the soldier's grave,
a five-year-old in pig tails, her family
gathered a row away,
where her grandfather rested.
Her Nanny's voice could be heard:
I'm coming Nathan!
which of course she wasn't,
though she said it every time they were there.

The girl remained fixated by this other
grave, barren, no rocks on a chipped
moss-covered footstone where only his rank
PVT could be seen. So the girl would kneel
to clear what she could, pick up a stone
from the walkway and gently place it
on his grave. She did that every time she was there.

One time her Nanny asked what she had been up to
when the girl returned to her mother's side:
*No one visits him, so I stop to say hello
and give him a rock.*

Her grandmother, not known for warmth,
looked down and said:
*I don't know where you got that from,
but God sees what you do.
Remember your old Nanny when she is gone.*

I'd love to see that kid again,
can't remember when she was here last.

Peace by Understanding

was the 1964 New York World's Fair
theme. It was a big deal. And more,
it took place in Queens. My mother splurged
and bought me a new pair of leather
saddle shoes just for this occasion.

Everybody posed by the Unisphere,
and who didn't love the animated
Abe Lincoln, or GE's Progressland?
But my all-time, hands-down favorite?
The African Pavilion.

Especially the huge banyan tree
whose branches embraced
and surrounded the Treehouse
restaurant and bar.
And I vividly remember the large,
cold bowl of peanut soup I was served.
Sweet savory memory, but still,
can't hold a candle to Suzy.

Suzy with her gigantic jet-black eyes,
brown square spots and very long,
black tongue that tickled my palm
as she gently ate the lettuce I fed her
when she stuck her head through
the window of the thatched roof.
And next to her, neck bent down,
stood her mother.

Years later, my mother smiled,
with her neck bent down.
My daughter, neck extended,
had a need to be heard,
despite how much she didn't listen.
It's always been like this. It was
always too much. Or not enough.

Memory 3

> with a nod to Wislawa Szymborska's "The Terrorist, He's Watching"

The virus has crossed our streets.
The distance between him and us grows small,
mask your face, latex coat your hands,
and even then, your ears and eyes are still exposed.

Clorox the counters, Windex the doors,
sanitize the canned goods, water bottles,
don't bring that delivery past the garage,
and remember to leave your shoes by the door.
Even then you are still exposed.

When I was a kid, my mother washed everything
that came into the house. Her weapons were simple:
a plain white washcloth and a bar of Ivory soap.
That large bar in the blue waxed paper wrapper
with a seam down the middle, to break into two.
Which she would do, with her small, always wet,
soapy hands. I never knew how she could bear
the water that hot—it was one of the few things
she did tolerate.

Go wash your hands and come back to me.
Upon your return you held them up high to her face,
I don't smell the soap, do it again.

And when you walked through her kitchen door
shoes came off, and she washed those too.
I think with the same white washcloth she used on everything else.
Even then, you were still exposed.

Which means trust no one. Let's face it, the devil
who was once an angel, even he now uses a drone.

Hey Mom,

You can only blame dementia for so much.
There's no denying you were mean to Dad and me.
More than four years since your demise and still I shudder
from my memory of the many Thanksgivings
that you denied us to gather as a family.
Then there were all those birthdays—especially Dad's 80th.
He was used to it though. I'm still working on it.

Did you know I would take him to Glen Patrick's
if his doctor's visit ended early?
That's where he taught me to drink vodka and cranberry—
you can't smell vodka on your breath.
And we all knew you were going to check his breath.
Hell, even the bartender knew.

You were never the one we ran to. I get it: Dad was tough
competition. Even the tenants in your building
spoke about him years after he died.
I don't even know if they posted a notice by the elevator
when you exited. I do know I should have checked.

You didn't feel loved. You had faults. You found faults.
But Mom, I always knew you loved us.
I should have told you that you were my best teacher.
Not because I listened to you. But because I didn't.
In your quest for the negative I discovered the positive.
And as dementia took control I found kindness.
Well done. Mom.

Dear Dad,

We seemed seamless. Until I re-read your letter—
the one you sent fifty years ago. I can almost hear the quick
click of your Royal typewriter and the crank of the roller
as you insert that Plains Indian stationary—
I know you really loved that cowboy and Indian stuff.

I suppose we were both disappointed with each other.
But there was no doubt about the love. Or our delight
in those many talks that went late into the night.
That slap when you were frustrated by my failure
to deal with mom—grandma told me later you were in tears.
So was I—for different reasons.

I never answered this letter. It took forty years just to re-read it
and realize how difficult it was for you to write.
Do I regret that? Not as much as the haunting thought
you might have waited for a response. You had no idea
that the letter became a treasure, top-shelved in my desk
as if it were a bottle of your eighteen-year-old single malt.

And I agree, you should have painted the castle with the moat.
But I never needed the knight climbing the ivy to the top
of the tower. I knew you would be there for me.

IV
Revelations

Revelation: *the act of disclosing; divine communication*

Tell Me a Story

Because I really need one
Final words not spoken
I was sanitized, covered, gloved,
He was hooked, tied, sedated
Sinatra piped in from Pandora
I clung to an old photo
Come back to me
Once Upon A Time
Then words were gone
Vocal chords constricted
We miss the smile, the warmth
The feel of his hand in mine

Mom wringing her hands,
eyes closing slowly.
A disinfected chill covered us
Couldn't look me in the eyes
Silence in surround-sound
Kodacolor slicing my palm
Come back to me
A family of four together
Jelly rings went sour
Tick-tick-tock, now no time
My sun, my father
My most unhappy ending.

Edna Sits on My Shoulder

No one else can see her,
but I know she is there.

She does whatever she desires.
She's pretty and petite, and cares

not if there is money for food
or rent—that's my problem.

No doubt she was always mean,
abusive—especially if you loved her,

and that worked well for her.
Not me—I would feel the guilt.

It would consume me, keep me
up all night long. Alcohol

and ice cream wouldn't help.
Penance must be my plan.

So she sits on my shoulder
in total disapproval.

Oh, there have been occasions
where I felt her slight nod,

but disappointment was never
far behind. Lots of disappointment.

Dead three years before I was born,
I still can't shrug her off.

Ode to an Incision

First slash
red splash
a grey gooey
baby cries.
Happy throbbing
life starts
to cut
penetrate
then scar.
Blue star bandaids
once did the trick
tears made gone
by a goodbye kiss.

Older incisions
were indecision
about precision.
It grows
purple pain
to match
the purple heart.
I can't fix this.
I can't fix this.
Constant worry
everything matters
no relief.
Hot salt tears
lots of loss.

Life.
You really do
kill me.

Dementia, a Pantoum

Dementia has its perks despite what has been said.
Short-term memory is highly over-rated and now
all your loved ones are back, have risen from the dead.
Slippers not shoes, bras be gone, comfort is what's on.

Short-term memory took flight, but really, it's all right.
Those old arguments and grudges? Departed. No more.
Slippers not shoes, bras be gone, housedress is on.
That overwhelming anger will release into a smile,

as old arguments and grudges slip further from view.
No more worries when our names evade you,
no angry eyes or vexation, a sweet smile emerges
each time you are willing to try something new.

Let our names at last escape you and do not worry,
you've earned the right to be left all alone.
So forget about chop suey, time to give sushi a go.
All that's now required is kindness with a nod

because you've earned the right to be left quite alone.
All your loved ones are back, have risen from the dead,
and kindness with a sweet nod is what's inside your head.
Dementia has its perks, despite what some have said.

Lokshen Kugel

No one makes kugel better than my daughter.
I hear my mother's voice every time I make this noodle pudding.
She must have been impressed that I separated the eggs,
and then beat the whites. Something she would never do.

Boil water, cook and drain broad egg noodles, mix in butter
and sugar. Stop here. Just for a moment to inhale the sweetness.
Then add cottage cheese, sour cream and those anointed egg
whites. Top with crumbled graham crackers and bake.

Still, I sold my mother short.
Never gave her credit for much of anything.
In her eyes, finally, I found trust. And her mouth,
the slight crook, a dementia give-away, gave me a smile.

Yes, she loved the kugel, served up with oven-roasted turkey,
fresh baked rolls and the smell of mulled cider on the stove.

It Begins with a Delmonico

fresh off the grill, seasoned with peppercorns,
kosher salt. Not purchased from the supermarket,
but direct from the best butcher.
Finish it off with a tab of herbed butter:
minced garlic, chopped fresh parsley—
life is simple, my father taught me.
And don't forget a good bottle of Pinot Noir.

I regret I never took my dad to Keens Steakhouse.
I could blame my mother for that, she was so easy
to blame, but it's on me. Keens is famous not only
for great meals but for countless pipes on ceiling rafters:
Roosevelt, the Babe, Belasco, Buffalo Bill. Yeah,
Dad would have been wowed by Buffalo Bill's pipe.
Good beef, great cowboy. What could be better?
And then there's the fresh baked bread: warm artisan loaf
wrapped in a cloth napkin on a wooden slab,
creamy butter and a sharp knife.

I still picture my Dad at our house, standing by the white brick
grill, a thick steak cooking over charcoal, the heat gray to red.
Sunday there would be steamers with broth, a Chesterfield
smoldering in a black plastic ash tray, ice cold
Miller within reach. Until chemo stole that sense
of smell and taste, which of course is the least of it
since it steals desire for a Delmonico first.
I could pour Dad any ale but would be happy if he could
finish his *Ensure* after I drove him back home.

It began with a Delmonico steak, fresh
from the grill, served with melted herbed butter.
Life can be simple. It's the now-empty chair that isn't.

חַמְסָה
Hamsa

Tattooed on the nape of her lovely long neck
during one of those drunken college nights,
my daughter, years later, wanted to remove it.
After all, you need more than a pretty amulet
to be strong.

Hamsa is a symbol for protection, calm, and perhaps
power to guard against the almighty evil eye.
It looks like an intricate hand, the hand of God,
five fingers spread out in an ornate design,
it has your back as it covers your head.
Reminds me of the time Afsar forcefully pushed his hand
to our car's windshield, when someone cut him off
on a blind curve. Five fingers outspread.
What does that mean Afsar?
Ah, memsahib can never use this, it means you had five fathers.

Now that is my idea of a protective hand.
A hamsa is the sweet symbol people trust to protect them
in strange lands, in the worst of times.
But have you ever heard someone swear it works?

I wear a garnet one, a beautiful bauble.
My son bought one for his sister when he was in Israel.
We hang them on the walls and we can tattoo them on our necks.
Pretty amulet. Pretty positive stuff.
Still, based on what I've seen, it's not *In God I trust*.
Depend on yourself.
Be strong.

Everybody Loves Somebody Sometime

My mother would yell at me from the kitchen
when I sat inches away from the TV screen,
*You'll ruin your eyes. I knew a girl
your age who went blind from that.*

But I couldn't get close enough.
The Dean Martin Show and the sight of Dean
as he slid down the pole, dressed in a tux,
with his hanky tucked in the chest pocket,
cigarette in hand and never an ash flicked.

Lean Dean and his lovely long legs.

Thursday nights I spent cross-legged
on the low pile of our brown tweed wall-
to-wall right next to Dad,
and in front of Dean.

Oh the songs they would sing,
What'll I Do?
My father loved that war-time song.
Dean and Dad, Vitalis perfect hair,
so smooth, so debonair.
Everybody Loves Somebody Sometime

Surrounded by *Golddiggers* and *Ding-a-Ling*
girls smothered in smoke and kisses,
sometimes the *Rat Pack* would appear:
Frank, Sammy, Peter and Joey.
Never Jerry.

Lean Dean and his Vegas rats—too cool.

For All We Know,
we may never meet again.
I loved when dad sang that one.
But my mother, still in the kitchen,
still cleaning up dinner dishes,
would emerge only when Dean would sing.

Now that's Amore.

Marital Aids

That's what my father called it. Eclectic items we cataloged
and sold in a small mail-order company we ran together.
Products to enhance, providing a service. Guaranteed.
Free returns and exchanges.

Once a customer came to my front door.
His penis ring didn't work. Couldn't help,
but gave him three gold-plated neck chains.
He didn't look thrilled, but perhaps
that was part of the problem.

I did insist we drop the switchblades.
Switched to the latest x-rated videos (which I viewed
while the kids were napping). Available in English
and Spanish. *Emotion Lotion* was included
as a bonus gift and more fun than a bottle of wine.

We had it all: ginseng, Spanish fly, vitamin supplements.
El Toro was popular with the guys: a penis pump
that promised big. PocketPal appalled my husband,
but had real purpose. Said so right on the box:
for when she isn't there.

The inflatable dolls came in three hair colors
with three usable holes. They also came with a permanent
look of horror, rather like Munch's *The Scream*
or my mother's face.

It's business Mom, we're helping people, providing service.
It's not martial arts. It's marital aids.

Miracle Mike

Of all the stories my father told, this was the one
I refused to believe.
Full faith when he brought a snake to school.
Great pride when he explained he got to class early,
unscrewed every typewriter, hid them in the closet,
before the first bell.
Somewhat appalled when he cut Penelope's long thick
braid to hang on his bike seat. Loved that he slept
with Red Buttons as they told jokes all night
in a Catskills motel. But this Miracle story
I just couldn't buy.

Fifty years later, ten years after his death, I found the story:

It happened by the hand of its owner, a Fruita, Colorado farmer:
Lloyd Olsen. Lloyd picked this chicken for dinner,
for his mother-in-law.
Maybe she made him nervous. Maybe Lloyd just had bad aim.
The cut was on an angle and the chicken lived. Headless.
It had an ear and could still cluck. Just not clearly.

Thanksgiving is near and the memory of Mike looms large
on my mind, this chicken who lived headless for eighteen months
and only died because the poor thing choked on a corn kernel
in a hotel in Phoenix.

Another lesson learned. Even Dad can't make this one up.
So best make sure all your cuts are clean.

My Father's Arms

The left one
wore a watch well.

While his right one
held us crook-close.

Arms that tenderly
touched Nat's knee

taught Brian the art of
bait and tackle.

Arms that reached for
war-wounded

and earned him
the beloved bronze star.

The Hyundai window
served as his arm rest.

Steer the wheel Dad.
Did you know

you were the force
behind our direction?

Or that your simple
was our complex?

Did you hear
the toast at Glen Patricks?

Those slim, firm arms
full of purpose.

I miss them
more than sunlight.

I kissed goodbye
My father's arms.

It's a Shade

I

Back in kindergarten
my favorite color was
black.
*Black is a shade,
not a color,
choose another.*
Dumb bitch.
Eager to please
I picked pink.

My bathroom
was carnation pink
ceramic square tiles:
sink, tub, toilet.
The metal wall hamper—
pink too.
Even that crocheted doll
that covered
our tissue box.

At least the room was trimmed in black.

Like a safe border
to have my tender talks
in my bathroom
with Grandpa Sam.
He thought I was great.
And pretty.
He made me smile.
Not an easy task
for a man who died
five days before
I was born.

II

When my daughter was six
she too loved our bathroom.
Gainsboro gray tiles,
pink toilet and tub,
round shag mat
bubble gum pink.
Black was not her favorite shade.

I would stand
on the other side
of the door and listen:
Two Cabbage Patch
bath babies splashing
giggling, whispering.
Until I entered,
then she turned:
Grandpa Bernie says hi.

Some little girls have unexpected power.

Lunatic

The backseat of my father's Buick
was where I met the moon
kneeling, gripping its head-
rest I would stare out
the rear window
riveted by her
ability to hang
over me
following
every block
stopping
when we
stopped
keeping
up as
Dad
sped
ahead
no man
in the
moon
no stupid
smiling face
just the moon
stealthy slim or
wholly pregnant
me spellbound—age
five and loving this drive
the backseat of my father's Buick

V
Conclusion

conclusion: *a final determination; result; end*

Who Are These People?

I.   The couple

Two photos placed side by side: the woman had grandmother's
eyes. She was tight-lipped, proper—unlike her Brooklyn
descendant.
The man looked younger (as they do) slightly cross-eyed, full
black-beard—a good face. He dressed like a laborer:
collarless shirt, wool vest and thick heavy coat.
Perhaps he was the owner of the confiscated shoe factory.

These photos all had her grandmother's name on the back.
But no one living knows who they are.

II.   The other man

had her father's lips, but this was not a handsome man:
a little like a Yiddish Abe Lincoln. He had large ears
that stood far out from his head. It was exaggerated
by his short, cropped hair, extremely deep-set eyes,
high cheek bones, weathered skin covering a thin,
sunken face. A face that completely intrigued her.

Were they victims or survivors?
Dead before anyone bothered numbering?

III.   Mother and child

Portrait of a young woman holding her baby, cheek-to-
cheek tight. The baby was beautiful: little pouty mouth,
a cupid's bow lip, her father would say. Tiny button nose
with clear, bright eyes. They were both dressed in hand-
knit sweaters.

Their eyes summoned her—not quite a plea,
more a recognition.
Or simply lack of hope.

Remember me. I had a name.

The Jewish Funeral

    after Wislawa Szymborska's "Funeral (II)"

"this is not a conservative service"
"no . . . no *tahara*? do they even bother to wash the body?"
"do you think she is laid out in linen or muslim?"
"linen suits her so much more"
"I understand they don't sit *shiva* using those cardboard boxes"
"guess they're uncomfortable enough having to stay together
for a few days"
"her parents are buried here too, but in the mausoleum"
"remember her mother completely freaked out at the uncles'
funeral?"
"the cranking of the lift to shove the coffin into the top tier,
she shrieked"
"yeah, but Harold assured her it will be great, they were on
the bottom level, the pricey one, and she would love it there"
"I'm not staying for the burial, the shoveling of
dirt on the coffin is too final"
"I understand she demanded a solid maple casket. He wanted
to put her in a veneer"
"hah. . . . no muslim and no veneer for that one"
"who is the rabbi doing the service? A good one I hope.
Not the one she worked for all those years?"
"is he still alive—he was older than her!"
"the daughter looks just like her"
"they all looked alike, but her kid is a half inch shorter,
which I remember really disturbed her"
"you know the grandmother described the son as an Adonis?"
"but did you see the husband? He looks quite shaken up by this"
"what do you think . . . six months
'til he finds someone to replace her?"
"enough—you're depressing me!"
"I love your shoes—the heel is not too high, but still sexy enough"
"Nordstrom Rack online—best selection and price"

In Appreciation for Her Final Observation

after Pamela Perkins-Frederick

Here's what I know: I drove my father home
from Memorial Sloan Kettering
on my 55th birthday.
And it was my best, my favorite gift.
Springtime. Sun shining. Car window open.
Dad's eyes closed.
Inhaling fresh air, feeling the sun's heat
on his weathered face, that still winning smile.

I'm not sure *I want to watch when I die.*
And I doubt I want to know how it will feel.
I think I want my senses sharp.
Let's face it, no one has the right
to dull them before death comes,
to take those final moments away,
like I did to my father.

You Pamela, face death like a warrior.
Maybe I might do the same, but I could not bear
my father's pain. The sting of our shared sorrow.
No, we dulled those senses with fentanyl,
then morphine—
that was his prelude to dust.

The Shadow Knows

I am so powerful that in my presence words are not needed,
I am that cloud passing over the sun, snuffing out the moon.

Truth is I cast myself over all that is beneath me. Let's face it—
I loom over your head, in front of your every step.

You might even be naïve enough to believe I am part of you,
trust this friend—far from it. And I steal, as often as possible.

I especially enjoy the theft of a canal reflection. The power
to obscure and steal the mirrored image of bloodroot and thistle.

There are songs about me, and puppet images created thanks
to me, but most of the time, I am more than dark—I am ominous.

Who needs language when I can take your breath away?
It is the shadow that I create to cross over. Close your eyes—

it only takes a moment—I can make a glorious day gone.
You can play with what you think is your shadow,

dance with it, sway back and forth, aim your camera above it,
but remember this: one day I will cast myself before you,
not behind.

I'll be the one to have that last word.

Silver Spoons

She kept them, all of them, sealed
in a Ziploc bag neatly tucked
in the silverware tray.
She didn't want them,
not at first, but he asked her,
when they both knew he was dying,
who will polish them when I'm gone?

How could this be important?
When she replied,
probably not me,
she thought she had shrugged it off.
But his question haunted, until finally,
ten years after, she opened the Ziploc.

Of course they had turned black,
but the tarnish did not hide
their beauty.
She gave her favorites
a purpose:
sugar bowls, jam pots,
petite espresso cups.

When she polished them,
they revealed themselves:
a grist mill, sunflowers with brass inlay,
a girl with long braids,
a building on the reverse side.
The one with a windmill that moved
she chose to grace her morning coffee.
The elk was used to scoop fig jam.

He knew her, so he knew it would come to this.

My Yizkor Moment

I buried my father in his Schnauzer print tie
and a favorite plaid sports jacket
that still smelled like him.
The funeral home didn't want
his soft beige-gray leather loafers.
He loved soft leather.

I buried my mother in a denim QVC
capri pants set which I bought
when her own clothes no longer fit.
Beneath that was a new floral flannel
house coat. Because that was all
she ever really wore. No underwear.
She hated underwear.

In the early morning hours
I think about their outfits as I get dressed.
First I select my shoes. I also love leather.
Then I consider the weather—
is it a flannel kind of day?
I can't help but wonder what outfit
will my kids select for me.

So tell me—what are you dying to wear?

Born in Brooklyn

but bred on the streets of Queens
in a compact square ranch house with mustard
aluminum siding and a large white awning
that covered the patio out back. The first house
to have outdoor speakers in our 'hood.

I am from the weeping willow tree by the pool
and the birch trees that lined their way to the kitchen
side door.

I am from minimal faith, free of obligation
along with a dedicated line of dementia—Nellie,
Helen and Evelyn—people who lost
most of their memories but didn't know it
and a grandmother who often requested:
remember me.

I come from a line of tailors, seamstresses
and furriers. I own their three sewing machines
and yet cannot thread a bobbin.

I am from patriotic parents who insisted I too
Stand up and salute no matter what.
Question little, follow doctor's directions,
marry later, but not too late to have a couple of kids.

Born in Brooklyn, I came from J&B (aka Jewish
Booze) with Sunday morning bagels.
From the long line of headstones at Cedar Park
Cemetery, the shared names, the secret suicides,
(they married into the family, so no worries),
and the No Exit sign at the corner of Block 5.

I am from the keepers of silver spoons
and ceramic shoes, the inheritor of buttons,
a glass ibex, the champleve vase and cartons
and cartons of black and white photos
that lie in rest, on metal shelves,
in the back room of the basement.

I am what's left of all of them.

About the Author

Julie Standig has studied at the *Unterberg Poetry Center,* participated in *Writer's Voice* and was an active member of a private workshop in NYC. A lifetime New Yorker, she now resides in Bucks County with her husband Ken and their Springer Spaniel, Dizzi. A proud member of the late and beloved Dr. Chris Bursk's springtime workshop, she continues to write with many of those talented poets. Julie has been published in *Alehouse Press, Arsenic Lobster* and *Covenant of the Generations, Sadie Girl Press, Schuylkill Journal Review, US1 Poets/Del Val* as well as the online journal, *Rats Ass Review, Silver Birch Press, MacQueen's Quinterly,* and *Poetry Super Highway.* Her first chapbook, *Memsahib Memoir,* was released in 2017 by Plan B Press. Her hope is that this collection will bring some humor and connection to others who sift through their own memories and objects. Look deep.

www.ingramcontent.com/pod-product-compliance
Lightning Source LLC
Chambersburg PA
CBHW022147160426
43197CB00009B/1462